B...
WARSHIPS
& AUXILIARIES

1992/93 Edition

THE ROYAL NAVY

The final disintegration of the Soviet empire in 1991 inevitably, and rightly, meant reductions in the strength of Western defences. Freed at long last of the nagging pressure of the massive Soviet military presence, after four and a half decades, the politicians and defence planners have the opportunity and time to consider a new strategy for Britain's armed forces. As we have, hopefully, learnt in recent years – we should expect the unexpected.

To be sure the task would not be an easy one. The next threat might be far removed from the Gulf. It might be in area where there were no friendly host nations to provide bases and facilities – as there had been during the Gulf war. Suddenly Britain's fast disappearing merchant fleet might be worth, almost, its weight in gold to provide sea lift of equipment, stores fuel, spares, ammunition and so on – even, maybe, for the troops themselves if the distances involved were too great, as was the case in the Falklands conflict, for the transport planes available; or refuelling stops and overflying rights were denied by other states. It is, though, significant that the new NATO Rapid Reaction Corps, formed after the Gulf War, and which Britain has been invited to lead, makes no mention at all of the need for seaborne transport if the need arises. Rather, it appears one of its purposes is to widen the scope for smaller NATO nations, particularly in southern Europe, to participate in a combined multi-national force. Whilst Britain is to take a leading rôle in the Land Forces, talk of disbanding the NATO Channel Command doesn't bode well for a major NATO rôle for our maritime forces.

Or, again, the dispute might be one of those long drawn out inconclusive confrontations, similar perhaps to the Icelandic "Cod Wars' of the 1950s-1970s or the Beira Patrol of the sixties, causing a drain on defence resources with little of the action needed from time to time to inspire the continuing support of MPs and public.

Looking back over the crises the British forces have had to face since 1945 the variety of possible scenarios is almost endless Few if any, could be foreseen. It would, therefore, be the height of folly to make preparations that do not allow tremendous flexibility.

Here naval forces have much to offer. As was shown in the South Atlantic in 1982 they can provide air cover; amphibious landing capability without reliance on any port; the transport, feeding and supplying in the field of a military expeditionary force and medical aid – all without recourse to shore support close at hand. This ability of naval forces to "live off their own backs" was amply demonstrated in the Gulf war when the RN ships, even including small "Hunt" class mine countermeasures vessels (MCMV), successfully operated for some 55 days supported only by the Royal Fleet Auxiliary.

But naval forces have a particularly unique quality. This is their ability to "loiter", "hover" or "maintain a presence" without infringing other states' sovereignty or, indeed, without necessarily appearing to offer a direct threat. Very few people indeed need to know they are "on station – over the horizon" – they can slip in and out almost without notice. A naval task group can remain in the area of a potential troublespot for weeks on end without committing the government to a course of action or the risk of reaction by others that would almost certainly occur were troops or aircraft to land in an area of dispute. No infantry battalion or air squadron in any case can long remain on foreign soil, even if the locals are friendly, without a staggering logistic backup of fuel, stores and spares in many instances needing to be brought in almost daily.

In outline these are some of the advantages naval forces can confer upon states that are both ready to use them and whose leaders have the imagination and grasp of the meaning of "sea power" to exploit them.

In Britain since 1945 there has been a kind of folklore that the massive reduction begun then and still continuing in the Royal Navy was necessary because (a) we had to show support for our allies in Europe against the giant steamroller that the Red Army appeared to be. (b) Because the threat was primarily on land the Navy had to be sacrificed to provide the money and manpower needed to maintain a standing army in continental Europe – something Britain had not had for centuries. In vain did a few more enlightened politicians and some service leaders (not all of them admirals, for Montgomery was one) point out that by far the biggest and most effective contribution Britain could make to Western Europe's security was at sea. Yet despite growing evidence of Moscow's awareness of NATO's vulnerability to attacks on her trans-Atlantic supply lines the maintenance of a huge (by British peacetime standards) army in Western Germany was the paramount requirement.

And then, suddenly, the whole thing started to unravel as the Warsaw Pact collapsed and many British Army weapons in Germany had the range to hit only targets in now friendly states – like Poland and Czechoslovakia.

The British government's reaction was swift, some might say too swift, in view of the continuing and dangerous power vacuum in the former Soviet empire. It was decreed that the Army was to be cut by almost a quarter from 156,000 to 116,00 men and women, although over a period of five years through 1995 – presumably allowing some rethinking if circumstances change in the meanwhile. Whether the Army can continue to sustain its present commitments with such a number is open to serious question and it is to be hoped events do not prove the government's calculations to have been wrong.

In some more woolly-headed political quarters reductions in defence spending were seen as giving the Treasury a chance to pay a "peace dividend" say to education and the health service. Those with a little more intimate knowledge of government finances are well aware a "peace" dividend is quite illusory and the saving, say, of £900m on the cost of supporting Army families in Germany and paying the wages of some 23,000 (mostly German) civil servants will not result in new hospitals or schools mushrooming throughout the UK.

Rather, the gradual relaxation of pressure on the defence budget from one particularly large consumer of funds in central Europe could, it might be supposed, give a little more latitude for consideration of other long-standing but unfunded projects. Instead we see

4

continuation of what for years has been known by defence planners as "salami slicing". The number of units in this programme is reduced … That programme is shelved for a year or two … Training with this weapon is cut to save money on annual ammunition demands … That piece of equipment is cancelled because 50% of what it is supposed to do can be done by existing equipment …

Often this kind of cost reduction would give senior officers virtually unanswerable dilemmas. Despite a requirement to steam at an economical speed, to save fuel, except when exercise or emergency needs dictated otherwise, one destroyer captain a few years ago decided to return from a NATO exercise in the Baltic at high speed. In this way his ship returned to Portsmouth in time for many of his ship's company to catch last trains to give them their first long weekend at home for months. The gesture was appreciated by many of the crew and may just possibly have influenced one or two to think again about quitting the Service prematurely so, perhaps, saving the high cost of training more replacements than might otherwise be necessary. Such considerations would be pooh-poohed by an accountant as being financially "unquantifiable" while the cost of the additional dieso fuel used could very easily be worked out.

Inhibiting the use of their imagination and developing leadership qualities among those in the Services may be only one tiny effect of "salami slicing". More seriously, its continuation into the 1990s in the wake of events on the international scene of the past three years is profoundly disturbing.

The purpose of this process in the 1970s and 1980s was so that Defence Ministers of both main parties could solemnly declare to Parliament and Britain's allies that she was maintaining all her capabilities – the five main pillars of the nation's defence policy – rather than opting out of one of them entirely. These pillars were: the nuclear deterrent; defence of the UK base; maintenance of British forces in the Eastern Atlantic (70% of the total in fact) and the capability for military intervention outside the NATO area. That British forces were increasingly *less* capable in supporting some of these pillars was hard for the outside observer to discern. Only in recent years, for example, has the all-Party Parliamentary Defence Committee been able to ascertain that RN and RAF maritime air contributions to NATO exercises have been steadily declining for some years because of too many commitments elsewhere.

But now, with one pillar (in central Europe) being greatly reduced in both money and manpower it absorbs, there would appear to be the time for a reappraisal of Britain's defence policy in considerable depth. Yet so far this does not appear to have happened to any extent. The planned number of destroyers and frigates, 40, will be 15 below the figure in 1983 and 25 below what the First Sea Lord at the time of the Falklands, Admiral Sir Henry Leach, considered were needed to meet then existing commitments (none of which has since disappeared). The number of submarines is being cut by roughly 25%, despite the enormous deterrent value in *conventional* war the nuclear powered Fleet submarine has demonstrated, as was shown also in 1982. Similarly, the number of MCMVs will have been cut in 18 months from 40 to around 32 by the beginning of this year, even though Britain's pre-eminence in mine warfare was so amply demonstrated in the Gulf. Without the RN MCMV's efforts there it seems fair to say that the reopening of Kuwait and the northern Gulf to commercial traffic would have been delayed for many weeks, if not months, with all the economic and political conse-

5

quences that might have followed.

It would, of course, be wrong to read a reappraisal of British defence policy simple as a shift in spending priorities. Rather, it is a question of reorientation in defence thinking putting "out of area" – as those parts of the globe beyond NATO's geographic confines are known – as the prime consideration in terms of policy, defence procurement and training.

Can this or that proposed new equipment meet hot, dusty and intense cold and humid conditions? Is the additional funding needed to give it such flexibility worth it in terms of the overall enhancement of "out of area" capabilities? Is self-protection with such things as armour to stop the most sophisticated anti-tank weapons known worth the added weight of a new armoured vehicle if this risks reducing its ability to use various landing platforms such as commercial roll-on roll-off ships? Do we need 200 plus multi-rôle aircraft designed to counter the best of the world's air defence systems – or 150 and 50 more rugged but less sophisticated tactical support aircraft able to aid ground and naval forces? Should we indeed be thinking in terms of a largely STOVL – Short Take Off and Vertical Landing – RAF in the next century? How many major airfields with long concrete runways might be available (and safe) in many Third World states without the addition also of defensive ground forces?

Operating at sea from ships is usually an annual occurence for the RAF's Harriers, its only aircraft, apart from helicopters, able to use an *Invincible* class carrier's flight deck. The number of occasions in peacetime that Army units are embarked for exercises in HM Ships in a year can be counted on the fingers of one hand. Germany and Northern Ireland commitments have seen that the soldiers have probably as little space in their programmes as do the RN's one operational assault ship and handful of RFA landing ships. In the Services themselves "jointery" – operating with one or both other services – is not the rarity it was maybe only 20 years ago. Nevertheless, such are the commitments faced by all three within their own single-service spheres of activity that "jointery" is far from being the norm. It should not be so and indeed with our numerically reduced forces in the near future we cannot afford for it to be. This is not to say Britain should go down the path taken by Canada with a single service for that experiment has, by all accounts, proved a disaster that the Canadians themselves are trying to unravel!

In the next decade there are two other considerations, particularly for the navy, that should feature as high on the agenda of the Whitehall policy makers as they did 20 years ago. These are what are rather vaguely termed "aid to the civil power" and "showing the flag". The former covers anything from relief work in areas of man-made or natural disasters, such as that provided by RFA *Fort Grange* with four Sea King helicopters of 826, 845 and 846 Naval Air Squadrons in Bangladesh last June after the disastrous cyclone, to the thankless task of maintaining anti-gun running patrols by "Bird" class patrol craft around Northern Ireland.

The latter essentially means visits by HM Ships to ports at home and overseas. Such visits may be linked directly to, say, an important exhibition or some Royal tour, or more often simply to places where (a) the Foreign Office has decided a British warship's visit would be diplomatically and maybe commercially advantageous or, (b) where British sailors are particularly welcome as visitors and tourists (again, though, Foreign Office "dip clear" – diplomatic clearance – has first to be obtained from the host state).

Sending RFA *Fort Grange* to Bangladesh was entirely appropriate – she could carry large quantities of relief stores and has a large helicopter deck and hangar. Yet she could only spend a couple of weeks off the stricken country whereas the US Navy for many weeks maintained a considerable naval aid force with ships being rotated as required. Such comparisons may mean little in view of the difference in sizes of the two navies. Yet it is not that long ago when questions were raised in Parliament and the press as to why it was, following a major earthquake in North Africa, Britain at first could only send a single coastal minesweeper and it was only days later a destroyer depot ship with urgently needed stores and technicians followed.

With the public perception that the Soviet threat (despite their continued SSN building

Soviet Victor Class. No longer a threat? 9-10 Soviet nuclear submarines are still being built each year.

programme) has largely vanished demands for such aid, most notably in the in the Third World (in other words "out of area") on the armed forces and particularly the Navy and the RAF's transport fleet seem bound to increase. This is likely to be as persuasive an argument as most, perhaps more than most, for the RN to maintain adequate heavy lift capabilities, ie amphibious ships and RFAs. At the time of writing the situation in Yugoslavia could well develop into HM Ships being sent to intervene in a humanitarian rôle.

"Showing the flag" is to some a rather emotive term. It conjures up Royal Marine bands playing "Sunset" against a tropical backdrop as white uniformed officers and civil dignitary and military guests stand solemnly clasping gin glasses. But the official cocktail party marking the arrival of one of HM Ships in a foreign port forms only a very small part of such visits and may be likened to the preview reception given by a commercial exhibitor to the local mayor and others. Certainly, a warship visit is about meeting people – and that works both ways with the ship open to the public and her crew playing local sports teams, maybe helping the local hospital or orphanage with some special project or just being seen around as tourists. All best summed up years ago by the British ambassador in Uruguay who told the ship's company of the frigate *Danae* that they had achieved more for Britain's prestige and to foster goodwill in their six-day visit than could have been achieved by six months of concentrated diplomatic and commercial effort.

From time to time it is reported that the recent visit of HMS *Nonsuch* to some small distant country was the first by one of HM Ships for 25 years – maybe much longer. Is it entirely surprising that in many of these small corners of the globe British influence – diplomatic as well as commercial – has vanished? Taken together these small states, islands, territories, could make a valuable market as, for example, the Japanese are fully aware. Are such factors taken into consideration by the cost-conscious Defence Ministry official, and even more so by his political masters, when denying approval for a 1000 mile diversion by a frigate to make such a visit? In recent years cost considerations and the lack of ships have made it seem this is too often so.

Perhaps the accountants are worried that on arrival on some far off shore "Jolly Jack" may actually enjoy himself. "Fun" doesn't appear in the index of the accountants manuals but, to an outsider looking in – and back – there appears to be a lack of this, almost dirty, three letter word. "There's no fun left" is a dangerous cry in the wardroom and messdecks of the Fleet …

There is scope now for tremendous re-thinking of Britain's aims in national security and the allocation of resources. The next three or four years will tell whether or not our leaders are prepared to seriously look once more to what the sea can offer us – or to cling more tightly to the so-called "European ideal" of ever closer integration of the 12 members of the European Community for whom the seas figure as a barrier – not a highway.

8

SHIPS OF THE ROYAL NAVY
Pennant Numbers

Ship	Pennant Number	Ship	Pennant Number
Aircraft Carriers		CHATHAM	F87
		BROADSWORD	F88
INVINCIBLE	R05	BATTLEAXE	F89
ILLUSTRIOUS •	R06	BRILLIANT	F90
ARK ROYAL	R07	BRAZEN	F91
		BOXER	F92
Destroyers		BEAVER	F93
		BRAVE	F94
BRISTOL •	D23	LONDON	F95
BIRMINGHAM	D86	SHEFFIELD	F96
NEWCASTLE	D87	COVENTRY	F98
GLASGOW	D88	CORNWALL	F99
EXETER	D89	AMAZON	F169
SOUTHAMPTON	D90	ACTIVE	F171
NOTTINGHAM	D91	AMBUSCADE	F172
LIVERPOOL	D92	ARROW	F173
MANCHESTER	D95	ALACRITY	F174
GLOUCESTER	D96	AVENGER	F185
EDINBURGH	D97	LANCASTER	F229
YORK	D98	NORFOLK	F230
CARDIFF	D108	ARGYLL	F231
		MARLBOROUGH	F233
Frigates		IRON DUKE	F234
		MONMOUTH	F235
CLEOPATRA	F28	MONTROSE	F236
SIRIUS	F40		
MINERVA	F45	**Submarines**	
JUNO	F52		
ARGONAUT	F56	OSIRIS	S13
ANDROMEDA	F57	ORACLE	S16
HERMIONE	F58	OTUS	S18
JUPITER	F60	OPOSSUM	S19
SCYLLA	F71	OPPORTUNE	S20
ARIADNE	F72	RESOLUTION	S22
CUMBERLAND	F85	REPULSE	S23
CAMPELTOWN	F86		

Ship	Pennant Number	Ship	Pennant Number
RENOWN	S26	ATHERSTONE	M38
REVENGE	S27	HURWORTH	M39
UPHOLDER	S40	BERKELEY	M40
UNSEEN	S41	QUORN	M41
URSULA	S42	BRINTON	M1114
UNICORN	S43	WILTON	M1116
COURAGEOUS	S50	IVESTON	M1151
TRENCHANT	S91	KELLINGTON	M1154
TALENT	S92	NURTON	M1166
TRIUMPH	S93	SHERATON	M1181
VALIANT	S102	SOBERTON	M1200
SCEPTRE	S104	SANDOWN	M101
SPARTAN	S105	INVERNESS	M102
SPLENDID	S106	CROMER	M103
TRAFALGAR	S107	WALNEY	M104
SOVEREIGN	S108	BRIDPORT	M105
SUPERB	S109	WAVENEY	M2003
TURBULENT	S110	CARRON	M2004
TIRELESS	S117	DOVEY	M2005
TORBAY	S118	HELFORD	M2006
SWIFTSURE •	S126	HUMBER	M2007
		BLACKWATER	M2008
Assault Ships		ITCHEN	M2009
		HELMSDALE •	M2010
FEARLESS	L10	ORWELL	M2011
INTREPID •	L11	RIBBLE •	M2012
		SPEY	M2013
Minesweepers & Minehunters		ARUN	M2014
BRECON	M29	**Patrol Craft**	
LEDBURY	M30		
CATTISTOCK	M31	PEACOCK	P239
COTTESMORE	M32	PLOVER	P240
BROCKLESBY	M33	STARLING	P241
MIDDLETON	M34	SENTINEL	P246
DULVERTON	M35	LEEDS CASTLE	P258
BICESTER	M36	REDPOLE	P259
CHIDDINGFOLD	M37	KINGFISHER	P260

Ship	Pennant Number	Ship	Pennant Number
CYGNET	P261	**Survey Ships & RN Manned Auxiliaries**	
ARCHER	P264		
DUMBARTON CASTLE	P265		
BITER	P270	BRITANNIA	A00
SMITER	P272	GLEANER	A86
PURSUER	P273	MESSINA	A107
ANGLESEY	P277	ROEBUCK	A130
ALDERNEY	P278	HECLA	A133
BLAZER	P279	HERALD	A138
DASHER	P280	POLAR CIRCLE	A176
ATTACKER	P281	IRONBRIDGE	A311
CHASER	P282	BULLDOG	A317
FENCER	P283	IXWORTH	A318
HUNTER	P284	BEAGLE	A319
STRIKER	P285	DATCHET	A357
PUNCHER	P291	CHALLENGER •	K07
CHARGER	P292		
RANGER	P293		
TRUMPETER	P294		
JERSEY	P295		
GUERNSEY	P297		
SHETLAND	P298		
ORKNEY	P299	• *Ships in reserve/long refit*	
LINDISFARNE	P300		

This book is updated and re-issued every *December*. Keep up to date … Don't miss the new edition.

Phone 0579 43663 for details.

HMS Resolution

RESOLUTION CLASS

Ship	Pennant Number	Completion Date	Builder
RESOLUTION	S22	1967	Vickers
REPULSE	S23	1968	Vickers
RENOWN	S26	1968	C. Laird
REVENGE	S27	1969	C. Laird

Displacement 8,400 tons (submerged) **Dimensions** 130m x 10m x 9m **Speed** 25 knots **Armament** 16 Polaris Missiles, 6 Torpedo Tubes **Complement** 147 (x 2).

Notes

These four nuclear-powered Polaris submarines are the United Kingdom's contribution to NATO's strategic nuclear deterrent. Despite the age of these vessels and, well publicised technical problems, one of these submarines is constantly on patrol and because of their high speed, long endurance underwater, and advanced sonar and electronic equipment they have little fear of detection.

Each submarine carries 16 Polaris two-stage ballistic missiles, powered by solid fuel rocket motors, 9.45 metres long, 1.37 metres diameter and weighing 12,700 kilogrammes with a range of 2,500 miles. The first of a new Vanguard Class was laid down in December 1986 and the second ordered in October 1987. They will carry the Trident D5 missile with a range of up to 6,000 miles. The first ship of the class (VANGUARD), is expected to enter service in 1994.

● LA PHOT BALL

HMS Valiant

VALIANT CLASS

Ship	Pennant Number	Completion Date	Builder
COURAGEOUS	S50	1971	Vickers
VALIANT	S102	1966	Vickers

Displacement 4,900 tons dived **Dimensions** 87m x 10m x 8m **Speed** 28 knots + **Armament** 6 Torpedo Tubes **Complement** 103.

Notes

These boats are capable of high underwater speeds and can remain on patrol almost indefinitely. They are able to circumnavigate the world without surfacing. Cost £24-£30 million each to build. CHURCHILL and DREADNOUGHT – the forerunners of this class – are awaiting disposal (by scrap or sinking) at Rosyth. CONQUEROR and WARSPITE at Devonport. Technical problems associated with their age have dictated that few saw operational service in 1991. COURAGEOUS and VALIANT have only seen limited sea service. Discussions continue regarding the safe disposal of these vessels.

SUBMARINES

13

● LA PHOT LEASK

HMS Sceptre

SWIFTSURE CLASS

Ship	Pennant Number	Completion Date	Builder
SCEPTRE	S104	1978	Vickers
SPARTAN	S105	1979	Vickers
SPLENDID	S106	1980	Vickers
SOVEREIGN	S108	1974	Vickers
SUPERB	S109	1976	Vickers
SWIFTSURE	S126	1973	Vickers

Displacement 4,500 tons dived **Dimensions** 83m x 10m x 8m **Speed** 30 knots + dived **Armament** 5 Torpedo Tubes **Complement** 116.

Notes
A follow-on class of ships from the Valiant Class. These submarines have an updated Sonar and Torpedo system. The class is transferring base port from Devonport to Faslane. SWIFTSURE (at Rosyth) is officially awaiting a decision on a refit or disposal but is unlikely to see further sea service and will doubtless be discarded in due course.

● PO PHOT NEWBURY

HMS Trafalgar

TRAFALGAR CLASS

Ship	Pennant Number	Completion Date	Builder
TRENCHANT	S91	1989	Vickers
TALENT	S92	1990	Vickers
TRIUMPH	S93	1991	Vickers
TRAFALGAR	S107	1983	Vickers
TURBULENT	S110	1984	Vickers
TIRELESS	S117	1985	Vickers
TORBAY	S118	1986	Vickers

Displacement 4,500 tons **Dimensions** 85m x 10m x 8m **Speed** 30 + dived **Armament** 5 Torpedo Tubes **Complement** 125.

Notes

Enhanced development of the Swiftsure Class. Quieter, faster and with greater endurance than their predecessors. Design option studies into a new SSN (based upon the Trafalgar Class) have been announced. Orders are expected to be placed in the mid to late 90's.

● OFFICIAL PHOTO

HMS Unseen

UPHOLDER CLASS

Ship	Pennant Number	Completion Date	Builder
UPHOLDER	S40	1989	Vickers
UNSEEN	S41	1991	Cammel Laird
URSULA	S42	1992	Cammel Laird
UNICORN	S43		Cammel Laird

Displacement 2,400 tons **Dimensions** 70m x 8m x 5m **Speed** 20 knots dived **Armament** 6 Torpedo Tubes: Sub Harpoon missile **Complement** 44.

Notes

A new class of conventionally powered submarines. UPHOLDER'S entry into service was delayed by industrial disputes and trials problems. Of 19 proposed vessels only the ships listed above will now be built. All vessels to be taken in hand at Devonport to rectify torpedo firing system.

● HMS GANNET

HMS Oracle

OBERON CLASS

Ship	Pennant Number	Completion Date	Builder
OSIRIS	S13	1964	Vickers
ORACLE	S16	1963	C. Laird
OTUS	S18	1963	Scotts
OPOSSUM	S19	1964	C. Laird
OPPORTUNE	S20	1964	Scotts

Displacement 2,410 tons (submerged) **Dimensions** 90m x 8m x 5m **Speed** 12 knots surface, 17 knots submerged **Armament** 8 Torpedo Tubes **Complement** 70.

Notes
The remainder of this class will be paid off within the next two years as the UPHOLDER Class enters service. ONYX, now at Birkenhead, opening as a tourist attraction in Spring 1992.

● OFFICIAL PHOTO

HMS Ark Royal

INVINCIBLE CLASS

Ship	Pennant Number	Completion Date	Builder
INVINCIBLE	R05	1979	Vickers
ILLUSTRIOUS	R06	1982	Swan-Hunter
ARK ROYAL	R07	1985	Swan-Hunter

Displacement 19,500 tons **Dimensions** 206m x 32m x 6.5m **Speed** 28 knots **Armament** Sea Dart Missile, 2 x 20mm guns, 3 Phalanx/Goalkeeper **Aircraft** 8 x Sea Harrier, 12 x Sea King **Complement** 900 + aircrews.

Notes
Manpower problems dictate that two ships are kept in the operational fleet, with the third being in refit or reserve. ILLUSTRIOUS is currently at Devonport and is expected to be in refit for two years.

● OFFICIAL PHOTOGRAPH

HMS Fearless

FEARLESS CLASS

Ship	Pennant Number	Completion Date	Builder
FEARLESS	L10	1965	Harland & Wolff
INTREPID	L11	1967	J. Brown

Displacement 12,500 tons, 19,500 tons (flooded) **Dimensions** 158m x 24m x 8m **Speed** 20 knots **Armament** 2 Sea Cat Missile Systems, 2 x 40mm guns, 4 x 30mm + 2 x 20mm (INTREPID only) 2 x Vulcan Phalanx (FEARLESS only) **Complement** 580.

Notes
Multi-purpose ships that can operate helicopters for embarked Royal Marine Commandos. 4 landing craft are carried on an internal deck and are flooded out when the ship docks down. INTREPID paid off in 1991. She is unlikely to see further sea service and is in reserve at Portsmouth with a maintenance crew of approximately 90 men. A decision was made in late 1991 that both vessels would be replaced in the Fleet.

ASSAULT SHIPS

HMS Bristol

BRISTOL CLASS (Type 82)

Ship	Pennant Number	Completion Date	Builder
BRISTOL	D23	1972	Swan Hunter

Displacement 6,750 tons **Dimensions** 154m x 17m x 7m **Speed** 30 knots +
Armament 1 x 4.5" gun, 1 Sea Dart Missile System, 4 x 30mm + 4 x 20mm guns
Complement 407.

Notes
Four ships of this class were ordered but three later cancelled when requirement for
large escorts for fixed wing aircraft carriers ceased to exist. Helicopter Deck provided
but no aircraft normally carried. Fitted for, but not with, Vulcan Phalanx. Paid off in June
1991. She is expected to replace KENT as a harbour training ship for Sea Cadets, once
funding is secured.

● OFFICIAL PHOTO

HMS Newcastle

SHEFFIELD CLASS
(Type 42) Batch 1 & 2

Ship	Pennant Number	Completion Date	Builder
BIRMINGHAM	D86	1976	C. Laird
NEWCASTLE	D87	1978	Swan Hunter
GLASGOW	D88	1978	Swan Hunter
EXETER	D89	1980	Swan Hunter
SOUTHAMPTON	D90	1981	Vosper T.
NOTTINGHAM	D91	1982	Vosper T.
LIVERPOOL	D92	1982	C. Laird
CARDIFF	D108	1979	Vickers

Displacement 3,660 tons **Dimensions** 125m x 15m x 7m **Speed** 29 knots **Armament** 1 x 4.5" gun, 4 x 20mm guns, Sea Dart Missile System: 2 x Phalanx, Lynx Helicopter, 6 Torpedo Tubes **Complement** 280 +.

Notes
Sister ships SHEFFIELD and COVENTRY lost in 1982 during the Falklands conflict. All ships are to be modernised with new radar and electronic warfare systems. SOUTHAMPTON completed repairs during 1991 to damage inflicted during a Gulf collision and will be operational again in 1992.

21

● OFFICIAL PHOTO

HMS Gloucester

SHEFFIELD CLASS
(Type 42) (Batch 3)

Ship	Pennant Number	Completion Date	Builder
MANCHESTER	D95	1983	Vickers
GLOUCESTER	D96	1984	Vosper T.
EDINBURGH	D97	1985	C. Laird
YORK	D98	1984	Swan Hunter

Displacement 4,775 tons **Dimensions** 132m x 15m x 7m **Speed** 30 knots + **Armament** 1 x 4.5" gun, 2 x Phalanx, 4 x 20mm guns Sea Dart missile system. Lynx helicopter, 6 Torpedo Tubes **Complement** 301.

Notes
"Stretched" versions of earlier ships of this class. Designed to provide area defence of a task force. Deck edge stiffening fitted to counter increased hull stress. EDINBURGH emerged from refit in late 1990 with new bow and forward mounted Phalanx. Studies continue on future frigate requirements – and a collaboration with likely European partners.

HMS Brilliant

BROADSWORD CLASS
(Type 22) (Batch 1)

Ship	Pennant Number	Completion Date	Builder
BROADSWORD	F88	1978 ✳	Yarrow
BATTLEAXE	F89	1980	Yarrow
BRILLIANT	F90	1981	Yarrow
BRAZEN	F91	1982	Yarrow

Displacement 3,860 tons **Dimensions** 131m x 15m x 6m **Speed** 29 knots **Armament** 4 Exocet Missiles, 2 Sea Wolf Missile Sytems, 4 x 30mm guns, 2 or 4 x 20mm guns, 6 Torpedo Tubes, 2 Lynx Helicopters **Complement** 224.

Notes
Successor to the successful Leander Class. Although capable of carrying 2 helicopters, only 1 normally embarked. These ships have been refitted with additional accommodation and classroom facilities and will deploy as Dartmouth Training Ships in a rota of two ships at a time.

✳ Sold to Brazilian Navy, named GREENHALGH (F46)

F
R
I
G
A
T
E
S

HMS Coventry

BROADSWORD CLASS
(Type 22) (Batch 2)

Ship	Pennant Number	Completion Date	Bulder
BOXER	F92	1983	Yarrow
BEAVER	F93	1984	Yarrow
BRAVE ●	F94	1985	Yarrow
LONDON ●	F95	1986	Yarrow
SHEFFIELD ●	F96	1987	Swan Hunter
COVENTRY ●	F98	1988	Swan Hunter

Displacement 4100 tons **Dimensions** 143m x 15m x 6m **Speed** 30 knots **Armament** 4 Exocet Missiles, 2 Sea Wolf Missile Systems, 4 x 30mm + 2 x 20mm guns, 6 Torpedo Tubes, 2 Lynx Helicopters **Complement** 273.

Notes
● Ships have enlarged hangar and flight deck. A Sea King can be, and is, carried in some ships of this class.

HMS Chatham

BROADSWORD CLASS
(Type 22) (Batch 3)

Ship	Pennant Number	Completion Date	Builder
CUMBERLAND	F85	1988	Yarrow
CAMPBELTOWN	F86	1988	C. Laird
CHATHAM	F87	1989	Swan Hunter
CORNWALL	F99	1987	Yarrow

Displacement 4,200 tons **Dimensions** 147m x 15m x 7m **Speed** 30 knots **Armament** 1 x 4.5" gun, 1 x Goalkeeper, 8 Harpoon, Seawolf, 4 x 30mm guns, 6 Torpedo Tubes, 2 Lynx or 1 Sea King Helicopter **Complement** 250.

Notes

General purpose gun and Goalkeeper system added to these ships as a direct result of lessons learned during Falklands conflict. All these ships have a major A/S and intelligence gathering capability. Cost £180 million each.

● OFFICIAL PHOTO

HMS Norfolk

DUKE CLASS (Type 23)

Ship	Pennant Number	Completion Date	Builder
LANCASTER	F229	1991	Yarrow
NORFOLK	F230	1989	Yarrow
ARGYLL	F231	1991	Yarrow
MARLBOROUGH	F233	1991	Swan Hunter
IRON DUKE	F234	1992	Yarrow
MONMOUTH	F235	Building	Yarrow
MONTROSE	F236	Building	Yarrow

Displacement 3,500 tons **Dimensions** 133m x 15m x 5m **Speed** 28 knots **Armament** Harpoon & Seawolf missile systems: 1 x 4.5" gun, 4 x 2 twin, magazine launched, Torpedo Tubes **Complement** 157.

Notes
WESTMINSTER, NORTHUMBERLAND and RICHMOND ordered (from Swan Hunter) in December 1989. Invitation to tender for 3 more ships issued in mid 1991.

● PO PHOT FERGUSON

HMS Juno

LEANDER CLASS

Ship	Pennant Number	Completion Date	Builder
✳ JUNO	F52	1967	Thornycroft
ARIADNE	F72	1972	Yarrow

Displacement 2,962 tons **Dimensions** 113m x 13m x 5m **Speed** 27 knots **Armament** 2 x 4.5" guns, 3 x 20mm guns, 1 Sea Cat Missile System, 1 Mortar Mk10, **Complement** 260.

Notes
JUNO (with a much reduced armament) is a training ship. ARIADNE was due for disposal during 1990 but will now run on until early 1992.She is the last steam propelled surface warship to be built for the Royal Navy.

✳ FEBRUARY, 1995 – 27 Sold to Spanish Breakers.

HMS Andromeda

LEADER CLASS
(Sea Wolf Conversions)

Ship	Pennant Number	Completion Date	Builder
✳ ANDROMEDA	F57	1968	HM Dockyard Portsmouth
HERMIONE	F58	1969	Stephen
JUPITER	F60	1969	Yarrow
SCYLLA	F71	1970	HM Dockyard Devonport

Displacement 2,962 tons **Dimensions** 113m x 13m x 5m **Speed** 27 knots **Armament** Sea Wolf System, 4 x Exocet Missiles, 2 x 20mm guns, 6TT, 1 Lynx helicopter **Complement** 260.

Notes
The refitting of these ships cost in the region of £70m – ten times their original cost – but modernisation programme curtailed from 10 to 5 ships. Small calibre armaments vary between individual ships. CHARYBDIS paid off in 1991. JUPITER will follow in early 1992.

✳ *1995, Sold to India Navy known as: INS KRISHNA.*

28

● OFFICIAL PHOTO   **HMS Sirius**

LEANDER CLASS
(Exocet Conversions)

Ship	Pennant Number	Completion Date	Builder
● CLEOPATRA	F28	1966	HMD Devonport
● SIRIUS	F40	1966	HMD Portsmouth
MINERVA	F45	1966	Vickers
● ARGONAUT	F56	1967	Hawthorn Leslie

Displacement 2,860 tons **Dimensions** 113m x 12m x 5m **Speed** 27 knots **Armament** 4 Exocet Missiles, 3 Sea Cat Missile Systems, 2 x 40mm guns, 6 Torpedo Tubes, 1 Lynx helicopter **Complement** 230.

Notes
● Ships have been refitted with Towed Array sonar and their armament reduced to 2 Sea Cat systems. Structural and mechanical problems are increasing the maintenance requirement for these elderly Leander class ships, but they have given excellent service during their long careers. PENELOPE and DANAE sold to Equador in 1991. MINERVA and CLEOPATRA for disposal early 1992.

29

● HMS OSPREY   **HMS Avenger**

AMAZON CLASS
(Type 21)

Ship	Pennant Number	Completion Date	Builder
AMAZON	F169	1974	Vosper T.
ACTIVE	F171	1977	Vosper T.
AMBUSCADE	F172	1975	Yarrow
ARROW	F173	1976	Yarrow
ALACRITY	F174	1977	Yarrow
AVENGER	F185	1978	Yarrow

Displacement 3,250 tons **Dimensions** 117m x 13m x 6m **Speed** 30 knots **Armament** 1 x 4.5" gun, 2 x 20mm guns, 4 Exocet Missiles, 1 Sea Cat Missile System, 1 Lynx helicopter, 6 Torpedo Tubes **Complement** 170.

Notes
Sister ships ANTELOPE and ARDENT lost during the Falklands conflict. All 6 ships have been given extra hull strengthening. This class (built to a commercial design, and subsequently sold to the Ministry of Defence) have received no major mid-life modernisation but continue to play a first class general purpose role in the fleet.

30

● OFFICIAL PHOTO

HMS Dulverton

MINE COUNTERMEASURES SHIPS (MCMV'S) BRECON CLASS

Ship	Completion Date	Pennant Number	Builder
BRECON	1980	M29	Vosper T.
LEDBURY	1981	M30	Vosper T.
CATTISTOCK	1982	M31	Vosper T.
COTTESMORE	1983	M32	Yarrow
BROCKLESBY	1983	M33	Vosper T.
MIDDLETON	1984	M34	Yarrow
DULVERTON	1983	M35	Vosper T.
BICESTER	1986	M36	Vosper T.
CHIDDINGFOLD	1984	M37	Vosper T.
ATHERSTONE	1987	M38	Vosper T.
HURWORTH	1985	M39	Vosper T.
BERKELEY	1988	M40	Vosper T.
QUORN	1989	M41	Vosper T.

Displacement 625 tonnes **Dimensions** 60m x 10m x 2.2m **Speed** 17 knots **Armament** 1 x 30mm + 2 x 20mm guns **Complement** 45.

Notes
The largest warships ever built of glass reinforced plastic. Designed to replace the Coniston Class – their cost (£35m each) has dictated the size of the class. Very sophisticated ships – and lively seaboats!

MCM VESSELS

● MARITIME PHOTOGRAPHIC — **HMS Carron**

FLEET MINESWEEPERS
RIVER CLASS

Ship	Pennant Number	Completion Date	Builder
WAVENEY	M2003	1984	Richards
CARRON	M2004	1984	Richards
DOVEY	M2005	1984	Richards
* M98 HELFORD SHAIBAL	M2006	1984	Richards
HUMBER	M2007	1985	Richards
BLACKWATER	M2008	1985	Richards
ITCHEN	M2009	1985	Richards
HELMSDALE	M2010	1985	Richards
ORWELL	M2011	1985	Richards
RIBBLE	M2012	1985	Richards
SPEY	M2013	1985	Richards
ARUN	M2014	1986	Richards

Displacement 850 tons **Dimensions** 47m x 10m x 3m **Speed** 14 knots **Armament** 1 x 40mm, 2 x GPMG **Complement** 30.

* BANGLEDESH NAVY (1995)

Notes

MCM ships serving with the RNR. BLACKWATER has an RN ships company and is in the Fishery Protection Squadron (FPS). Built to commercial specifications with steel hulls. Designed for 'sweeping in deep water. Orders for four more of this class were expected in 1987 but were not confirmed. HELMSDALE and RIBBLE laid up (at Portsmouth) in 1991 as a defence economy.

HMS Nurton

CONISTON CLASS

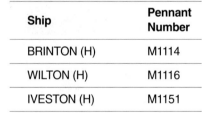

Ship	Pennant Number	Ship	Pennant Number
BRINTON (H)	M1114	NURTON (H)	M1166
WILTON (H)	M1116	SHERATON (H)	M1181
IVESTON (H)	M1151	SOBERTON (S)	M1200
KELLINGTON (H)	M1154		

Displacement 425 tons **Dimensions** 46m x 9m x 3m **Speed** 15 knots **Armament** 1 x 40mm gun **Complement** 29/38.

Notes
120 of this class were built in the early 50s but most have now been sold overseas or scrapped. They have fulfilled many roles over the years and have given excellent service. WILTON, built of glassfibre in 1973, was the world's first 'plastic' warship. She is a training ship for BRNC Dartmouth. Ships marked (S) are Minesweepers – (H) Minehunters.

● OFFICIAL PHOTO

HMS Sandown

SANDOWN CLASS

Ship	Pennant Number	Completion Date	Builder
SANDOWN	M101	1989	Vosper T.
INVERNESS	M102	1991	Vosper T.
CROMER	M103	1991	Vosper T.
WALNEY	M104	1992	Vosper T.
BRIDPORT	M105		Vosper T.

Displacement 450 tons **Dimensions** 53m x 10m x 2m **Speed** 13 knots **Armament** 1 x 30mm gun **Complement** 34.

Notes
A new class dedicated to a single mine hunting role. Propulsion is by vectored thrust and bow thrusters. Up to 15 more ships were planned, but the 7 due to be ordered in 1991 were cancelled. Six similar ships are being built for Saudi Arabia.

HMS Dumbarton Castle

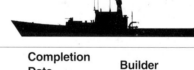

CASTLE CLASS

Ship	Pennant Number	Completion Date	Builder
LEEDS CASTLE	P258	1981	Hall Russell
DUMBARTON CASTLE	P265	1982	Hall Russell

Displacement 1,450 tons **Dimensions** 81m x 11m x 3m **Speed** 20 knots **Armament** 1 x 40mm gun **Complement** 40.

Notes
These ships have a dual role – that of fishery protection and offshore patrols within the limits of UK territorial waters. Unlike the Island Class these ships are able to operate helicopters – including Sea King aircraft. Trials have been conducted to assess the suitability of these ships as Minelayers. DUMBARTON CASTLE currently on long term deployment to the Falklands Islands with her ships' company rotating every four months.

35

PATROL VESSELS

HMS Alderney

ISLAND CLASS

Ship	Pennant Number	Completion Date	Builder
ANGLESEY	P277	1979	Hall Russell
ALDERNEY	P278	1979	Hall Russell
JERSEY	P295	1976	Hall Russell
GUERNSEY	P297	1977	Hall Russell
SHETLAND	P298	1977	Hall Russell
ORKNEY	P299	1977	Hall Russell
LINDISFARNE	P300	1978	Hall Russell

Displacement 1,250 tons **Dimensions** 60m x 11m x 4m **Speed** 17 knots **Armament** 1 x 40mm gun **Complement** 39.

Notes
Built on trawler lines these ships were introduced to protect the extensive British interests in North Sea oil installations and to patrol the 200 mile fishery limit.

JSPRS HONG KONG

HMS Plover

PEACOCK CLASS

Ship	Pennant Number	Completion Date	Builder
PEACOCK	P239	1983	Hall Russell
PLOVER	P240	1983	Hall Russell
STARLING	P241	1984	Hall Russell

Displacement 700 tons **Dimensions** 60m x 10m x 5m **Speed** 28 knots **Armament** 1 x 76mm gun **Complement** 31.

Notes
The first warships to carry the 76mm Oto Melara gun. They are used to provide an ocean going back-up to the Marine Department of the Hong Kong Police. The Government of Hong Kong has paid 75% of the building and maintenance costs of these vessels. Sister ships SWALLOW and SWIFT returned to UK in 1988 and were sold (Oct 88) to the Irish Navy after only 3 years RN service.

● HMS NEPTUNE

SENTINEL CLASS

Ship	Pennant Number	Completion Date	Builder
SENTINEL	P246	1975	Husumwerft

Displacement 1710 tons **Dimensions** 60m x 13m x 4m **Speed** 14 knots **Armament** 2 x 40mm **Complement** 26.

Notes

Formerly the Oil Rig support vessel Seaforth Saga. Employed in the Clyde area on Submarine escort duties – and "marking" of Soviet vessels off N. Ireland. It is expected this ship will be sold in 1992

HMS Blazer

COASTAL TRAINING CRAFT
ARCHER CLASS

Ship	Pennant Number	Completion Date	Builder
ARCHER	P264	1985	Watercraft
BITER	P270	1985	Watercraft
SMITER	P272	1986	Watercraft
PURSUER	P273	1988	Vosper
BLAZER	P279	1988	Vosper
DASHER	P280	1988	Vosper
PUNCHER	P291	1988	Vosper
CHARGER	P292	1988	Vosper
RANGER	P293	1988	Vosper
TRUMPETER	P294	1988	Vosper

Displacement 43 tonnes **Dimensions** 20m x 6m x 1m **Speed** 20 knots **Armament** Nil **Complement** 14.

Notes
In service with RNR divisions and RN University units. TRUMPETER and RANGER deployed to Gibraltar in 1991 to replace HART and CORMORANT (sold locally).

39

HMS Cygnet

BIRD CLASS

Ship	Pennant Number	Completion Date	Builder
REDPOLE	P259	1970	Fairmile
KINGFISHER	P260	1975	R. Dunston
CYGNET	P261	1976	R. Dunston

Displacement 190 tons **Dimensions** 37m x 7m x 2m **Speed** 21 knots **Complement** 24.

Notes
REDPOLE commissioned into the Royal Navy in 1985 after service as an RAF search and rescue craft.

● OFFICIAL PHOTO   **HMS Fencer**

ATTACKER CLASS

Ship	Pennant Number	Completion Date	Builder
ATTACKER	P281	1983	Allday
CHASER	P282	1984	Allday
FENCER	P283	1983	Allday
HUNTER	P284	1983	Allday
STRIKER	P285	1984	Allday

Displacement 34 tons **Dimensions** 20m x 5m x 1m **Speed** 24 knots **Complement** 11.

Notes

Seamanship & Navigational training vessels for the Royal Naval Reserve & University RN Units. Based on a successful design used by HM Customs. ATTACKER, HUNTER and STRIKER deployed to Cyprus for security patrol duties in late 1990. Due for disposal in March 1992. CHASER on loan to RNXS until July 1992. FENCER for disposal spring 1992

41

● R.M. POOLE

HMS Messina

MANLY CLASS

Ship	Pennant Number	Completion Date	Builder
MESSINA	A107	1982	R. Dunston

Displacement 127 tons **Dimensions** 25m x 6m x 2m **Speed** 10 knots **Complement** 9/13.

Notes
Very similar to the RMAS/RNXS tenders. MANLY, MENTOR and MILBROOK were sisters and employed on training duties attached to HMS RALEIGH. All three paid off in late 1991 and are for sale. MESSINA is a training ship for Royal Marines based at Poole. IXWORTH (A318), IRONBRIDGE (A311) and DATCHET (A357) are all former RMAS tenders now flying the White Ensign as diving tenders.

HMS Roebuck

ROEBUCK CLASS

Ship	Pennant Number	Completion Date	Builder
ROEBUCK	A130	1986	Brooke Marine

Displacement 1500 tonnes **Dimensions** 64m x 13m x 4m **Speed** 15 knots **Complement** 47.

Notes
Was due to replace HECLA in the Survey fleet until the latter reprieved in 1987 for further service. Fitted with the latest fixing aids and sector scanning sonar.

● OFFICIAL PHOTO

HMS Herald

HECLA CLASS

Ship	Pennant Number	Completion Date	Builder
HECLA	A133	1965	Yarrow
HERALD	A138	1974	Robb Caledon

Displacement 2,733 tons **Dimensions** 79m x 15m x 5m **Speed** 14 knots **Complement** 115.

Notes
Able to operate for long periods away from shore support, these ships and the smaller ships of the Hydrographic Fleet collect the data that is required to produce the Admiralty Charts and publications which are sold to mariners worldwide. HERALD is an improved version of the earlier ships. HECATE for sale at Portsmouth.

HMS Beagle

BULLDOG CLASS

Ship	Pennant Number	Completion Date	Builder
BULLDOG	A317	1968	Brooke Marine
BEAGLE	A319	1968	Brooke Marine

Displacement 1,088 tons **Dimensions** 60m x 11m x 4m **Speed** 15 knots **Complement** 39.

Notes
Designed to operate in coastal waters. Both have been extensively refitted to extend hull life. FOX was sold for commercial service in December 1988, but enquiries have been made regarding chartering her back into the Hydrographic Fleet. FAWN paid off during 1991 and is expected to be sold to another Government department.
GLEANER (A86) is a small inshore survey craft based at Portsmouth.

HMS Challenger

SEABED OPERATIONS VESSEL

Ship	Pennant Number	Completion Date	Builder
CHALLENGER	K07	1984	Scott Lithgow

Displacement 6,400 tons **Dimensions** 134m x 18m x 5m **Speed** 15 knots **Complement** 185.

Notes

CHALLENGER was equipped to find, inspect and, where appropriate, recover objects from the seabed at greater depths than is currently possible. She was designed with a saturation diving system enabling up to 12 men to live in comfort for long periods in a decompression chamber amidships, taking their turns to be lowered in a diving bell to work on the seabed. Also fitted to carry out salvage work. Paid off in November 1990 as a defence economy. No suitable buyer has been found and discussions continue regarding her future. All saturation diving systems have now been removed from the vessel.

● OFFICIAL PHOTO

HMY Britannia

ROYAL YACHT

Ship	Pennant Number	Completion Date	Builder
BRITANNIA	A00	1954	J. Brown

Displacement 5,280 tons **Dimensions** 126m x 17m x 5m **Speed** 21 knots **Complement** 250.

Notes

Probably the best known ship in the Royal Navy, BRITANNIA was designed to be converted to a hospital ship in time of war but this conversion was not made during the Falklands crisis. Is available for use in NATO exercises when not on 'Royal' business. Normally to be seen in Portsmouth Harbour when not away on official duties. The only seagoing ship in the RN commanded by an Admiral.

47

SPECIAL SHIPS

N.C. HALL

HMS Polar Circle

ICE PATROL SHIP

Ship	Pennant Number	Completion Date	Builder
POLAR CIRCLE	A176	1990	Ulstein-Hatlo

Displacement 5,129 tons **Dimensions** 91m x 17.9m x 6.5m **Speed** 14.9 knots **Armament** Small arms **Aircraft** 2 Lynx **Complement** 113.

Notes
Chartered for seven months in late 1991 to replace HMS ENDURANCE in the South Atlantic.

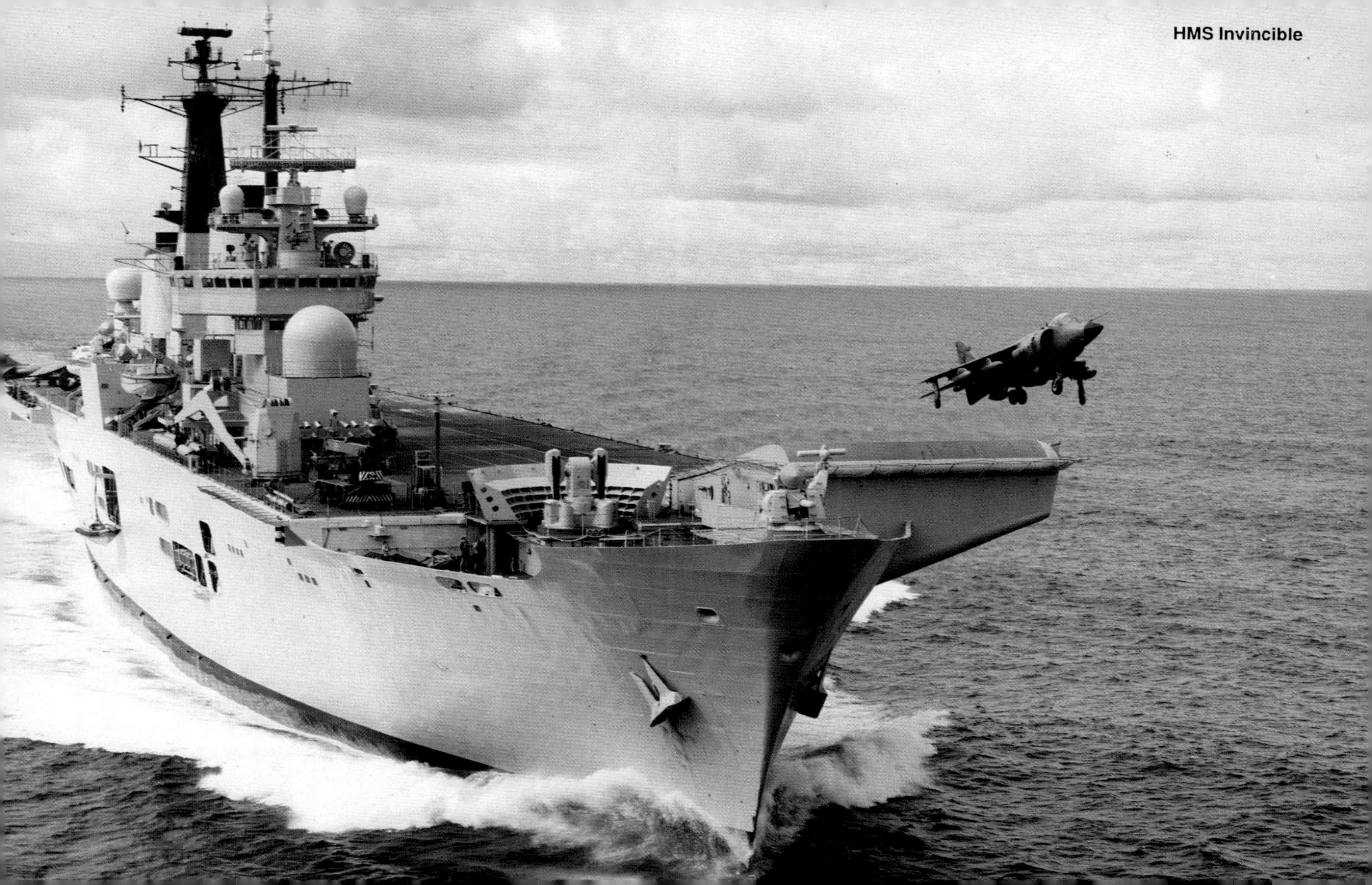
HMS Invincible

HMS Fearless

West Indies Guardship – HMS Arrow

F173

F95

HMS London (and Brazen)

HMS Polar Circle

M30

Bowing Out ... (l to r) HM Ships Jupiter, Hermione and Juno

THE ROYAL FLEET AUXILIARY

The Royal Fleet Auxiliary Service (RFA) is a civilian manned fleet owned and operated by the Ministry of Defence. Its main task is to supply warships of the Royal Navy at sea with fuel, food, stores and ammunition which they need to remain operational while away from base. With so few bases overseas which can be guaranteed in time of tension – let alone during any conflict it has become vital, over the years, that everything from the smallest nut and bolt to a complete aero engine is taken on any naval deployment away from our coasts. The lack of that nut and bolt could well stop a ship in its tracks – literally. Increasingly, the service also provides aviation support for the Royal Navy – together with amphibious support and secure sea transport for army units and their equipment.

With a Navy shrinking in size – and more reductions planned – it is inevitable that economies in size are being investigated within the service. In recent years vessels have paid off – or been reduced to reserve. Support ships are, however, vital if British Forces are to be supported at any distance from our shores.

With a limited size, specialist, Fleet the RFA has the minimum number of ships to cope with its present tasks – let alone the unexpected.

With an ever diminishing merchant service and an RFA Fleet looking decidedly "old" it will be interesting to see what effect the international situation will have in Whitehall. One cannot for ever go on "just getting by".

SHIPS OF THE ROYAL FLEET AUXILIARY
Pennant Numbers

Ship	Pennant Number	Ship	Pennant Number	Ship	Pennant Number
TIDESPRING	A75	ARGUS	A135	FORT GEORGE	A388
BRAMBLELEAF	A81	GREEN ROVER	A268	RESOURCE	A480
BAYLEAF	A109	GREY ROVER	A269	REGENT	A486
ORANGELEAF	A110	BLUE ROVER	A270	SIR BEDIVERE	L3004
OAKLEAF	A111	GOLD ROVER	A271	SIR GALAHAD	L3005
OLWEN	A122	BLACK ROVER	A273	SIR GERAINT	L3027
OLNA	A123	FORT GRANGE	A385	SIR PERCIVALE	L3036
OLMEDA	A124	FORT AUSTIN	A386	SIR TRISTRAM	L3505
DILIGENCE	A132	FORT VICTORIA	A387		

● OFFICIAL PHOTO

RFA Olmeda

'OL' CLASS

Ship	Pennant Number	Completion Date	Builder
OLWEN	A122	1965	Hawthorn Leslie
OLNA	A123	1966	Hawthorn Leslie
OLMEDA	A124	1965	Swan Hunter

Displacement 36,000 tons **Dimensions** 197m x 26m x 10m **Speed** 19 knots **Complement** 92.

Notes
These ships can operate up to 3 Sea King helicopters. Dry stores can be carried – and transferred at sea – as well as a wide range of fuel, aviation spirit and lubricants. All these vessels have now been refitted to bring them up to modern standards – and to increase their 'lifespan' – possibly to the turn of the century.

RFA Tidespring refuels HMS Charybdis

TIDE CLASS

Ship	Pennant Number	Completion Date	Builder
TIDESPRING	A75	1963	Hawthorn Leslie

Displacement 27,400 tons **Dimensions** 177m x 22m x 10m **Speed** 18 knots **Armament** 2 x 20mm guns **Complement** 98.

Notes

Built to fuel warships at sea in any part of the world. Strengthened for ice operations. A hangar and flight deck provides space for two Sea King helicopters if required. Was due to be "retired early" during 1982/83 but reprieved for Falklands crisis. She has been "reprieved" for further service many times, but is now expected to pay off for sale or scrap in early 1992.

TANKERS

RFA Gold Rover

ROVER CLASS

Ship	Pennant Number	Completion Date	Builder
GREEN ROVER ●	A268	1969	Swan Hunter
GREY ROVER	A269	1970	Swan Hunter
BLUE ROVER	A270	1970	Swan Hunter
GOLD ROVER	A271	1974	Swan Hunter
BLACK ROVER	A273	1974	Swan Hunter

Displacement 11,522 tons **Dimensions** 141m x 19m x 7m **Speed** 18 knots **Armament** 2 x 20mm guns **Complement** 49/54

Notes
Small Fleet Tankers designed to supply HM ships with fresh water, dry cargo and refrigerated provisions as well as a range of fuel and lubricants. Helicopter deck but no hangar. ● In reserve at Portsmouth, her sale to Indonesia was being negotiated at the end of 1991

● PO PHOT FERGUSON

RFA Oakleaf

LEAF CLASS

Ship	Pennant Number	Completion Date	Builder
BRAMBLELEAF	A81	1980	Cammell Laird
BAYLEAF	A109	1982	Cammell Laird
ORANGELEAF	A110	1982	Cammell Laird
OAKLEAF	A111	1981	Uddevalla

Displacement 37,747 tons **Dimensions** 170m x 26m x 12m **Speed** 14.5 knots
Complement 60.

Notes

All are ex merchant ships. BRAMBLELEAF is owned by MOD (N), the remainder are on bare boat charter. OAKLEAF (ex OKTANIA) differs from the other ships of the class which are all commercial Stat 32 tankers. At 49,310 tons she is the largest vessel in RFA/RN service. APPLELEAF taken over by the Royal Australian Navy (as HMAS Westralia) in late 1989.

RFA Fort Austin

FORT CLASS I

Ship	Pennant Number	Completion Date	Builder
FORT GRANGE	A385	1978	Scott Lithgow
FORT AUSTIN	A386	1979	Scott Lithgow

Displacement 23,384 tons **Dimensions** 183m x 24m x 9m **Speed** 20 knots **Complement** 201, (120 RFA, 36 RNSTS & 45 RN).

Notes

Full hangar and maintenance facilities are provided and up to four Sea King helicopters can be carried for both the transfer of stores and anti-submarine protection of a group of ships. Both ships can be armed with 4 x 20mm guns mounted on the Scot platforms. Both are fitted with 3" Chaff Systems.

● HARLAND & WOLFF

RFA Fort Victoria

FORT CLASS II

Ship	Pennant Number	Completion Date	Builder
FORT VICTORIA	A387	1992	Harland & Wolff
FORT GEORGE	A388	Building	Swan Hunter

Displacement 31,500 tons **Dimensions** 204m x 30m x 9m **Speed** 20 knots
Armament 4 x 30mm guns, Sea Wolf Missile System **Complement** 100 (RFA), 24
civilians, 32 RN and up to 112 aircrew.

Notes
These ships can operate 3 Sea King helicopters. A "one stop" replenishment ship with
the widest range of armaments, fuel and spares carried. Maintenance facilities for helicopters onboard. Delays at the builder will mean plans for FORT VICTORIA to enter
service in 1992 will not be met. She is now due to enter service in 1993 – her sister ship
12 months later..

63

● HMS OSPREY

RFA Regent

REGENT CLASS

Ship	Pennant Number	Completion Date	Builder
RESOURCE	A480	1967	Scotts
REGENT	A486	1967	Harland & Wolff

Displacement 22,890 **Dimensions** 195m x 24m x 8m **Speed** 21 knots **Armament** 2 x 20mm guns **Complement** 182, (RFA 112, RNSTS 37, RN 11).

Notes

The widest range of naval armament stores are carried onboard plus a limited range of general naval stores and food. When the Wessex 5 was withdrawn from service in April 1987 both ships lost their permanently embarked helicopter but they retain full flight deck facilities. RESOURCE reverted to Reserve (Preservation by Operation) status at Rosyth in November 1991.

● LA PHOT GIBSON

RFA Sir Geraint

LANDING SHIPS
SIR LANCELOT CLASS

Ship	Pennant Number	Completion Date	Builder
SIR BEDIVERE	L3004	1967	Hawthorn
SIR GALAHAD	L3005	1987	Swan Hunter
SIR GERAINT	L3027	1967	Stephen
SIR PERCIVALE	L3036	1968	Hawthorn
SIR TRISTRAM	L3505	1967	Hawthorn

Displacement 5,550 tons **Dimensions** 126m x 18m x 4m **Speed** 17 knots **Armament** Can be fitted with 2 x 40mm guns in emergency **Complement** 65, SIR GALAHAD (8,451 tons. 140m x 20m **Complement** 58).

Notes
Manned by the RFA but tasked by the Army, these ships are used for heavy secure transport of stores – embarked by bow and stern doors – and beach assault landings. Can operate helicopters from tank deck if required. SIR LANCELOT sold for commercial service in 1989.

RFA Diligence

Ship	Pennant Number	Completion Date	Builder
DILIGENCE	A132	1981	Oresundsvarvet

Displacement 5,814 tons **Dimensions** 120m x 12m x 3m **Speed** 15 knots **Armament** 2 x 20mm **Complement** RFA 40. RN Personnel – approx 100.

Notes

Formerly the M/V Stena Inspector purchased (£25m) for service in the South Atlantic. Accommodation is provided for a 100 man Fleet Maintenance Unit. Her deep diving complex was removed and workshops added. Has given valuable support to a wide range of warships in the Falklands and Gulf.

RFA Argus

Ship	Pennant Number	Completion Date	Builder
ARGUS	A135	1981	Cantieri Navali Breda

Displacement 28,081 tons (full load) **Dimensions** 175m x 30m x 8m **Speed** 18 knots **Armament** 4 x 30mm, 2 x 20mm **Complement** 254 (inc 137 Air Group) **Aircraft** 6 Sea King, 12 Harriers can be carried in a "ferry role".

Notes
Formerly the M/V CONTENDER BEZANT taken up from trade during the Falklands crisis. Purchased in 1984 (£13 million) for conversion to an 'Aviation Training Ship'. A £50 million re-build was undertaken at Belfast from 1984-87. Undertook rapid conversion in October 1990 to "Primary Casualty Reception Ship" (Hospital Ship!) for service in the Gulf. These facilities remain "mothballed" on board for activation if required.

ROYAL MARITIME
AUXILIARY SERVICE

The Royal Maritime Auxiliary Service Fleet is administered by the Director of Marine Services (Naval) to whom the Captains of the Ports and Resident Naval Officers at the various Naval Bases are mainly responsible for the provision of Marine Services to the Royal Navy. The Fleet continues to be reduced as the size of the Royal Navy has itself shrunk. It is still however responsible for over 400 hulls ranging from ocean going ships to small harbour lighters. The Fleet also includes 15 Army Range safety craft, 12 RAF Maritime Craft and over 20 MOD Police boats.

Ships of the RMAS, which can be seen at work in all the Naval Bases throughout the United Kingdom and at Gibraltar, are easily identified by their black hulls, buff coloured superstructure and funnels, and by the RMAS flag, which is a blue ensign defaced in the fly by a yellow anchor over two wavy lines. Pennant numbers are painted only on those vessels that are normally employed outside harbour limits.

SHIPS OF
THE ROYAL MARITIME AUXILIARY SERVICE
Pennant Numbers

Ship	Pennant Number	Ship	Pennant Number
CAMERON	A72	EXPLOIT	A167
MELTON	A83	LABRADOR	A168
MENAI	A84	KITTY	A170
MEON	A87	LESLEY	A172
MILFORD	A91	LILAH	A174
ALSATIAN	A106	MARY	A175
FELICITY	A112	EDITH	A177
MAGNET	A114	HUSKY	A178
LODESTONE	A115	MASTIFF	A180
CAIRN	A126	IRENE	A181
TORRENT	A127	SALUKI	A182
TORRID	A128	ISABEL	A183
DALMATION	A129	SALMOOR	A185
TORNADO	A140	SALMASTER	A186
TORCH	A141	SALMAID	A187
TORMENTOR	A142	POINTER	A188
TOREADOR	A143	SETTER	A189
WATERMAN	A146	JOAN	A190
FRANCES	A147	JOYCE	A193
FIONA	A148	GWENDOLINE	A196
FLORENCE	A149	SEALYHAM	A197
GENEVIEVE	A150	HELEN	A198
GEORGINA	A152	MYRTLE	A199
EXAMPLE	A153	SPANIEL	A201
EXPLORER	A154	NANCY	A202
DEERHOUND	A155	NORAH	A205
DAPHNE	A156	LLANDOVERY	A207
LOYAL HELPER	A157	LAMLASH	A208
SUPPORTER	A158	LECHLADE	A211
LOYAL WATCHER	A159	BEE	A216
LOYAL VOLUNTEER	A160	LOYAL MODERATOR	A220
LOYAL MEDIATOR	A161	FORCEFUL	A221
ELKHOUND	A162	NIMBLE	A222
EXPRESS	A163	POWERFUL	A223
GOOSANDER	A164	ADEPT	A224
POCHARD	A165	BUSTLER	A225
KATHLEEN	A166	CAPABLE	A226

Ship	Pennant Number	Ship	Pennant Number
CAREFUL	A227	CRICKLADE	A381
FAITHFUL	A228	ARROCHAR	A382
CRICKET	A229	CLOVELLY	A389
COCKCHAFER	A230	CRICCIETH	A391
DEXTEROUS	A231	GLENCOE	A392
GNAT	A239	DUNSTER	A393
SHEEPDOG	A250	FINTRY	A394
LYDFORD	A251	GRASMERE	A402
LADYBIRD	A253	CROMARTY	A488
MEAVEY	A254	DORNOCH	A490
CICALA	A263	ROLLICKER	A502
SCARAB	A272	HEADCORN	A1766
AURICULA	A285	HEVER	A1767
ILCHESTER	A308	HARLECH	A1768
INSTOW	A309	HAMBLEDON	A1769
FOXHOUND	A326	LOYAL CHANCELLOR	A1770
BASSET	A327	LOYAL PROCTOR	A1771
COLLIE	A328	HOLMWOOD	A1772
CORGI	A330	HORNING	A1773
FOTHERBY	A341	WATERSHED	Y18
FELSTED	A348	WATERSPOUT	Y19
ELKSTONE	A353	OILPRESS	Y21
FROXFIELD	A354	OILSTONE	Y22
EPWORTH	A355	OILWELL	Y23
ROYSTERER	A361	OILBIRD	Y25
WHITEHEAD	A364	OILMAN	Y26
FULBECK	A365	WATERCOURSE	Y30
ROBUST	A366	WATERFOWL	Y31
NEWTON	A367	MOORHEN	Y32
WARDEN	A368	MOORFOWL	Y33
KINTERBURY	A378		

● I. BIGNELL

RMAS Roysterer

ROYSTERER CLASS

Ship	Pennant Number	Completion Date	Builder
ROYSTERER	A361	1972	C.D. Holmes
ROBUST	A366	1974	C.D. Holmes
ROLLICKER	A502	1973	C.D. Holmes

G.R.T. 1,036 tons **Dimensions** 54m x 12m x 6m **Speed** 15 knots **Complement** 21.

Notes
Built for salvage and long range towage, a role they only fulfil infrequently. They are, however, used for various "deepwater" trials for MOD research departments.

TUGS

71

RMAS Adept

HARBOUR TUGS
TWIN UNIT TRACTOR TUGS (TUTT'S)

Ship	Pennant Number	Completion Date	Builder
FORCEFUL	A221	1985	R. Dunston
NIMBLE	A222	1985	R. Dunston
POWERFUL	A223	1985	R. Dunston
ADEPT	A224	1980	R. Dunston
BUSTLER	A225	1981	R. Dunston
CAPABLE	A226	1981	R. Dunston
CAREFUL	A227	1982	R. Dunston
FAITHFUL	A228	1985	R. Dunston
DEXTEROUS	A231	1986	R. Dunston

G.R.T. 375 tons **Dimensions** 39m x 10m x 4m **Speed** 12 knots **Complement** 9.

Notes
The principle harbour tug in naval service. CAPABLE is at Gibraltar.

RMAS Dalmatian

DOG CLASS

Ship	Pennant Number	Ship	Pennant Number
ALSATION	A106	POINTER	A188
CAIRN •	A126	SETTER	A189
DALMATIAN	A129	SEALYHAM	A197
DEERHOUND	A155	SPANIEL	A201
ELKHOUND	A162	SHEEPDOG	A250
LABRADOR	A168	FOXHOUND	A326
HUSKY	A178	BASSET	A327
MASTIFF	A180	COLLIE •	A328
SALUKI	A182	CORGI	A330

G.R.T. 152 tons **Dimensions** 29m x 8m x 4m **Speed** 12 knots **Complement** 5.

Notes
General harbour tugs – all completed between 1962 and 1972.
• No longer tugs. Refitted as trials vessels for service at Kyle of Lochalsh.
The long term replacement of these vessels is now a priority. Two Trident submarine berthing tugs were ordered in Dec 1991 for delivery in 1993. Two vessels will be chartered in the interim (for VANGUARD sea trials).

RMAS Edith

IMPROVED GIRL CLASS

Ship	Pennant Number	Ship	Pennant Number
DAPHNE	A156	EDITH	A177

G.R.T. 75 tons **Speed** 10 knots **Complement** 4.

Notes
All completed 1971-2. DAISY, DORIS, CHARLOTTE and CHRISTINE sold 1989 and DOROTHY in 1990.

RMAS Norah

IRENE CLASS

Ship	Pennant Number	Ship	Pennant Number
KATHLEEN	A166	ISABEL	A183
KITTY	A170	JOAN	A190
LESLEY	A172	JOYCE	A193
LILAH	A174	MYRTLE	A199
MARY	A175	NANCY	A202
IRENE	A181	NORAH	A205

G.R.T. 89 tons **Speed** 8 knots **Complement** 4.

Notes
Known as Water Tractors these craft are used for basin moves and towage of light barges.

75

RMAS Felicity

FELICITY CLASS

Ship	Pennant Number	Ship	Pennant Number
FELICITY	A112	GENEVIEVE	A150
FRANCES	A147	GEORGINA	A152
FIONA	A148	GWENDOLINE	A196
FLORENCE	A149	HELEN	A198

G.R.T. 80 tons **Speed** 10 knots **Complement** 4.

Notes
Water Tractors – completed in 1973; FRANCES, FLORENCE and GENEVIEVE completed 1980.

● M. FISHWICK

RMAS Newton

RESEARCH VESSEL

Ship	Pennant Number	Completion Date	Builder
NEWTON	A367	1976	Scotts

G.R.T. 2,779 tons **Dimensions** 99m x 16m x 6m **Speed** 15 knots **Complement** 39

Notes
An underwater research vessel with a limited cable laying capability.
The Trials ship RMAS WHITEHEAD (A364) laid up (at Devonport) in long term reserve. A possible rôle for Defence Research Agencies is under investigation.

TRIALS SHIPS

RMAS Auricula

TEST & EXPERIMENTAL SONAR TENDER

Ship	Pennant Number	Completion Date	Builder
AURICULA	A285	1981	Ferguson Bros

G.R.T. 981 tons **Dimensions** 52m x 11m x 3m **Speed** 12 knots **Complement** 20.

Notes
Employed on evaluation work of new sonar equipment that may equip RN ships of the future. Based as Portland.

RMAS Arrochar

ARMAMENT STORES CARRIERS

Ship	Pennant Number	Completion Date	Builder
KINTERBURY	A378	1980	Appledore SB
ARROCHAR	A382	1981	Appledore SB

G.R.T. 1,357 tons **Dimensions** 64m x 12m x 5m **Speed** 14 knots **Complement** 19.

Notes
2 holds carry Naval armament stores, ammunition and guided missiles. Both vessels vary slightly. ARROCHAR (ex ST GEORGE) taken over in late 1988 from the Army and is the only operational vessel. KINTERBURY in reserve at Portsmouth. THROSK sold to Equador 30.11.91.

● MARITIME PHOTOGRAPHIC

RMAS Bee

INSECT CLASS

Ship	Pennant Number	Completion Date	Builder
BEE	A216	1970	C.D. Holmes
CRICKET	A229	1972	Beverley
COCKCHAFER	A230	1971	Beverley
GNAT	A239	1972	Beverley
LADYBIRD	A253	1973	Beverley
CICALA	A263	1971	Beverley
SCARAB	A272	1973	Beverley

G.R.T. 279 tons **Dimensions** 34m x 8m x 3m **Speed** 10.5 knots **Complement** 7-9.

Notes
CRICKET and SCARAB are fitted as Mooring Vessels and COCKCHAFER as a Trials Stores Carrier – remainder are Naval Armament carriers.

● M LENNON

XSV Loyal Helper

LOYAL CLASS

Ship	Pennant Number	Ship	Pennant Number
XSV LOYAL HELPER	A157	XSV LOYAL MEDIATOR	A161
XSV SUPPORTER	A158	XSV LOYAL MODERATOR	A220
XSV LOYAL WATCHER	A159	XSV LOYAL CHANCELLOR	A1770
XSV LOYAL VOLUNTEER	A160	XSV LOYAL PROCTOR	A1771

G.R.T. 112 tons **Dimensions** 24m x 6m x 3m **Speed** 10.5 knots **Complement** 24.

Notes
All these craft are operated by the Royal Naval Auxiliary Service (RNXS) – men (and women) – who, in time of emergency, would man these craft for duties as port control vessels.

● MARITIME PHOTOGRAPHIC

RMAS Froxfield

(TYPE A, B & X) TENDERS

Ship	Pennant Number	Ship	Pennant Number
MELTON	A83	FULBECK	A365
MENAI	A84	CRICKLADE	A381
MEON	A87	CLOVELLY	A389
MILFORD	A91	CRICCIETH	A391
LLANDOVERY	A207	GLENCOE	A392
LAMLASH	A208	DUNSTER	A393
LECHLADE	A211	FINTRY	A394
LYDFORD	A251	GRASMERE	A402
MEAVEY	A254	CROMARTY	A488
ILCHESTER ●	A308	DORNOCH	A490
INSTOW ●	A309	HEADCORN	A1766
FOTHERBY	A341	HEVER	A1767
FELSTED	A348	HARLECH	A1768
ELKSTONE	A353	HAMBELDON	A1769
FROXFIELD	A354	HOLMWOOD	A1772
EPWORTH	A355	HORNING	A1773

G.R.T. 78 tons **Dimensions** 24m x 6m x 3m **Speed** 10.5 knots **Complement** 4/5.

Notes

All completed since 1971 to replace Motor Fishing Vessels. Vessels marked ● are diving tenders. Remainder are Training Tenders, Passenger Ferries, or Cargo Vessels. GLENCOE to RNR at Southampton 1991. DENMEAD for disposal.

● MARITIME PHOTOGRAPHIC

XSV Express

COASTAL TRAINING CRAFT
EXAMPLE CLASS

Ship	Pennant Number	Completion Date	Builder
XSV EXAMPLE	A153	1985	Watercraft
XSV EXPLORER	A154	1985	Watercraft
XSV EXPRESS	A163	1988	Vosper T
XSV EXPLOIT	A167	1988	Vosper T

Displacement 43 tons **Dimensions** 20m x 6m x 1m **Speed** 20 knots **Armament** Nil
Complement 14

Notes
Training vessel for the RNXS. In wartime would be used within ports/anchorages on port control duties. XSV CHASER – see page 41.

RMAS Oilwell

COASTAL OILERS
OILPRESS CLASS

Ship	Pennant Number	Completion Date	Builder
OILPRESS	Y21	1969	Appledore Shipbuilders
OILSTONE	Y22	1969	Appledore Shipbuilders
OILWELL	Y23	1969	Appledore Shipbuilders
OILBIRD	Y25	1969	Appledore Shipbuilders
OILMAN	Y26	1969	Appledore Shipbuilders

G.R.T. 362 tons **Dimensions** 41m x 9m x 3m **Speed** 11 knots **Complement** 5.

Notes
Employed as Harbour and Coastal Oilers.

RMAS Watershed

WATER CARRIERS
WATER CLASS

Ship	Pennant Number	Completion Date	Builder
WATERSHED	Y18	1967	Drypool Eng Co
WATERSPOUT	Y19	1967	Drypool Eng Co
WATERCOURSE	Y30	1974	Drypool Eng Co
WATERFOWL	Y31	1974	Drypool Eng Co
WATERMAN	A146	1978	R. Dunston

G.R.T. 263 tons **Dimensions** 40m x 8m x 2m **Speed** 11 knots **Complement** 5.

Notes
Capable of coastal passages, these craft normally supply either demineralised or fresh water to the Fleet within port limits. WATERSIDE sold to Equador 30.11.91. The hulk of the former WATERFALL is used as a salvage training hulk on the Clyde.

● MARITIME PHOTOGRAPHIC

RMAS Magnet

DEGAUSSING VESSELS
MAGNET CLASS

Ship	Pennant Number	Completion Date	Builder
MAGNET	A114	1979	Cleland
LODESTONE	A115	1980	Cleland

G.R.T. 828 tons **Dimensions** 55m x 12m x 4m **Speed** 14 knots **Complement** 9.

Notes
LODESTONE is currently operational (on the Clyde). MAGNET in reserve (Portsmouth).

RMAS Torrent

TORPEDO RECOVERY VESSELS (TRV'S)
TORRID CLASS

Ship	Pennant Number	Completion Date	Builder
TORRENT	A127	1971	Cleland SB Co
TORRID	A128	1972	Cleland SB Co

G.R.T. 550 tons **Dimensions** 46m x 9m x 3m **Speed** 12 knots **Complement** 14.

Notes
A stern ramp is built for the recovery of torpedoes fired for trials and exercises. A total of 32 can be carried. (TORRID currently in reserve (Clyde) will be sold in early 1992.)

T R V' s

RMAS Tormentor

TORNADO CLASS

Ship	Pennant Number	Completion Date	Builder
TORNADO	A140	1979	Hall Russell
TORCH	A141	1980	Hall Russell
TORMENTOR	A142	1980	Hall Russell
TOREADOR	A143	1980	Hall Russell

G.R.T. 560 tons **Dimensions** 47m x 8m x 3m **Speed** 14 knots **Complement** 13.

Notes
TORCH is based at Portland, TORMENTOR at Plymouth – remainder on the Clyde. All vessels have had suitable rails fitted to enable them to operate as exercise minelayers.

RMAS Salmoor

MOORING & SALVAGE VESSELS
SAL CLASS

Ship	Pennant Number	Completion Date	Builder
SALMOOR	A185	1985	Hall Russell
SALMASTER	A186	1986	Hall Russell
SALMAID	A187	1986	Hall Russell

Displacement 2200 tonnes **Dimensions** 77m x 15m x 4m **Speed** 15 knots **Complement** 17.

Notes

Multi-purpose vessels designed to lay and maintain underwater targets and moorings and undertake a wide range of salvage tasks.

M
S
V'
s

RMAS Goosander

WILD DUCK CLASS

Ship	Pennant Number	Completion Date	Builder
GOOSANDER	A164	1973	Robb Caledon
POCHARD	A165	1973	Robb Caledon

G.R.T. 900 tons* **Dimensions** 58mm x 12m x 4m **Speed** 10 knots **Complement** 18.

Notes
Vessels capable of carrying out a wide range of duties laying moorings and heavy lift salvage work. 200 tons can be lifted over the bow. POCHARD in reserve (Portsmouth).

RMAS Moorfowl

MOOR CLASS

Ship	Pennant Number	Completion Date	Builder
MOORHEN	Y32	1989	McTay Marine
MOORFOWL	Y33	1989	McTay Marine
CAMERON	A72	1991	Richard Dunston

Displacement 518 tons **Dimensions** 32m x 11m x 2m **Speed** 8 knots
Complement 10

Notes
Powered mooring lighters for use within harbour limits. (MOORHEN at Portsmouth, MOORFOWL at Devonport). CAMERON is similar but is employed as an Underwater Trials & Experimental vessel at Rosyth.

RMAS Warden

WARDEN CLASS

Ship	Pennant Number	Completion Date	Builder
WARDEN	A368	1989	Richards

Displacement 626 tons **Dimensions** 48m x 10m x 4m **Speed** 15 knots **Complement** 11.

Notes
Accepted into service Nov 1989 to replace DOLWEN as the Range Mooring Vessel for RAE Aberporth (S. Wales). Based at Pembroke Dock.

In October 1989 the RMAS took over the running of the Army Range Safety Group. This consisted of 15 craft most of which are only 15m boats. There are however two 24m craft the details of which are:

Ship	Pennant Number	Completion Date	Builder
FALCONET (ex Alfred Herring VC)	Y01	1983	James & Stone
PETARD (ex Michael Murphy VC)	Y02	1983	James & Stone

G.R.T. 70 tons **Dimensions** 24m x 5.5m x 2.5m **Speed** 21 knots **Complement** 6.

Their primary tasks are range surveillance and clearance, target towing for weapon attacks and the recovery of Sonabouys, maritime weapons and training devices in coastal range areas.

Further to the above DMS(N) took over Management of the RAF Marine Craft on 1 February 1991.
The RAF Fleet consists of the following craft:

SEAL & SEAGULL
LRRSC (Long Range Recovery and Support Craft)

G.R.T. 159 tons **Dimensions** 37m x 7m x 2m **Speed** 21 knots.

These craft are similar to HMS REDPOLE.

SPITFIRE, HALIFAX, HAMPDEN, HURRICANE, LANCASTER & WELLINGTON
RTTL's (Rescue Target Towing Launch)

G.R.T. 71 tons **Dimensions** 22m x 5.6m x 1.6m **Speed** 21 knots

All the craft are at present operated by James Fisher and Sons. The craft are split between bases at Invergordon, Great Yarmouth, Holyhead and RAF Mountbatten (Plymouth). The craft are employed on Target Towing, SAR, various trials and Weapon recovery.

HMAV Ardennes

ARMY LANDING CRAFT
LCL CLASS (LANDING CRAFT LOGISTIC)

Vessel	Pennant Number	Completion Date	Builder
HMAV Ardennes	L4001	1977	Brooke Marine
HMAV Arakan	L4003	1978	Brooke Marine

Displacement 1,050 tons **Dimensions** 72m x 15m x 2m **Speed** 10 knots **Complement** 36.

Notes
Designed to carry up to 520 tonnes of cargo, overside loaded, or up to Five Chieftain tanks – Ro Ro loaded, reducing to 254 tonnes for beaching operations, through bow doors. Principal roles are maintenance of the Royal Artillery Range Outer Hebrides and in support of Amphibious Operations and Exercises.

RCTV Abbeville

RCL CLASS
(RAMPED CRAFT LOGISTIC)

Vessel	Pennant Number	Completion Date	Builder
RCTV Arromanches	L105	1981	Brooke Marine
RCTV Antwerp	L106	1981	Brooke Marine
RCTV Andalsnes	L107	1984	James & Stone
RCTV Abbeville	L108	1984	James & Stone
RCTV Akyab	L109	1984	James & Stone
RCTV Aachen	L110	1986	McTay Marine
RCTV Arezzo	L111	1986	McTay Marine
RCTV Agheila	L112	1987	McTay Marine
RCTV Audemer	L113	1987	McTay Marine

Displacement 165 tons **Dimensions** 33m x 8m x 1.5m **Speed** 9 knots **Complement** 6.

Notes
Smaller – "all purpose" landing craft capable of carrying up to 100 tons. In service in coastal waters around Cyprus, Hong Kong & UK.

Appleby

SEA CADET VESSELS

FLEET TENDERS 63 DESIGN

Ship	Pennant Number	Ship	Pennant Number
ABERDOVEY	Y10	BEDDGELERT	A100
ABINGER	Y11	BIBURY	A103
ALNMOUTH	Y13	APPLEBY	A383

Displacement 117 tons **Dimensions** 24m x 5m x 3m **Speed** 10.5 knots.

Notes

'A' craft were built by Isaac Pimblott, Northwich; 'B' craft by J.S. Doig, Grimsby.

'A' craft are allocated to the Sea Cadet Corps. ABERDOVEY, Southern Area, Portsmouth based; ABINGER, Eastern Area, Grimsby based; ALNMOUTH, North West Area, Liverpool based; APPLEBY, South West Area, based at Portland (summer) and Bristol (winter).

BEDDGELERT is attached to HMS CAROLINE (Belfast). BIBURY presently carries the name SULTAN VENTURER and operates from PORTSMOUTH for HMS SULTAN.

MOD(N) also own and maintain MFV's 16, 96 and 816 and ex IMS PAGHAM for the S.C.C.

British Aerospace Sea Harrier

Variants: FRS 1 (FRS 2 undergoing development).
Role: Short take off, vertical landing (STOVL) fighter, reconnaissence and strike aircraft.
Engine: 1 x 21,500lb thrust Rolls Royce PEGASUS 104, 106 turbojet.
Span 25' 3" **length** 47' 7" **height** 12' 0" **Max weight** 26,200lb.
Max speed Mach 1.2 **Crew** 1 pilot.
Avionics: Blue Fox pulse radar. (To be replaced by the Blue Vixen pulse doppler radar in the FRS 2).
Armament: SEA EAGLE air to surface missiles. SIDEWINDER air to air missiles. (FRS 2 to carry the new Anglo/US AMRAAM radar guided air to air missiles). 2 x 30mm Aden cannons with 120 rounds per gun in detachable pods, one either side of the lower fuselage. 1 fuselage centreline and 4 underwing hardpoints. The inner wing stations are capable of carrying 2,000lb of stores and are plumbed for drop tanks. The other positions can carry stores up to 1,000lb in weight. Possible loads include 1,000lb, 500lb or practice bombs; BL 755 cluster bombs, Lepus flares, 190 or 100 gallon drop tanks. A single F95 camera is mounted obliquely in the nose for the reconnaissance role. The prototype FRS 2 first flew in September 1988 and sea trials took place in October 1990.
Squadron Service: 800, 801 and 899 squadrons in commission.
Notes: During 1992, 800 squadron will be embarked in HMS INVINCIBLE and 801 in HMS ARK ROYAL. 899 squadron is responsible for the training of replacement pilots and the development of tactics and is normally shore based at RNAS YEOVILTON. In a period of tension it could embark to reinforce the embarked air groups in the carriers.

Westland SEA KING

Developed for the Royal Navy from the Sikorsky SH3D, the basic Sea King airframe is used in three different roles. The following details are common to all:
Engines: 2 x 1600shp Rolls Royce Gnome H 1400 – 1 free power turbines.
Rotor Diameter 62' 0" **Length** 54' 9" **Height** 17' 2" **Max Weight** 21,400lb **Max Speed** 125 knots.
The 3 versions are:-

HAS 5/6

The HAS6 has improved sonics, deeper dipping active sonar and Racal "Orange Crop 2" ESM
Roles: Anti-submarine search and strike. SAR. Transport.
Crew: 2 pilots, 1 observer and 1 aircrewman.
Avionics: MEL Sea Searcher radar; Plessey Type 195 variable depth active/passive sonar. GEC LAPADS passive sonobuoy analyses. Marconi Orange Crop passive ESM equipment.
Armament: 4 fuselage hardpoints capable of carrying STINGRAY torpedoes or depth charges. Various flares, markers, grenades and sonobuoys can be carried internally and hand launched. A 7.62mm machine gun can be mounted in the doorway.
Squadron Service: 771, 810, 814, 819, 820 and 826 squadrons in commission equipped with Mk6, 706 with Mk5.
Notes: The Sea King has been the backbone of the Fleet Air Arm's anti-submarine force since 1970. 706 is the advanced training squadron at RNAS CULDROSE. 810 is an operational training squadron with the capability to embark to reinforce the front line. During 1992, 814 squadron will be embarked in HMS INVINCIBLE and 820 in HMS ARK ROYAL. 819 is shore based at PRESTWICK and 826 provides Flights deployed in frigates and RFAs. The HAS 6 retains a noteable SAR capability which is frequently demonstrated in the south west approaches.

AEW 2

Role: Airborne Early Warning. **Crew:** 1 pilot and 2 observers.
Avionics: Thorn/EMI Searchwater radar. Marconi Orange Crop passive ESM equipment.
Armament: Nil.
Squadron Service: 849 HQ, 849A and 849B flights in commission.
Notes: Used to detect low flying aircraft trying to attack aircraft carrier battle groups under shipborne radar cover. Can also be used for surface search utilising its sophisticated, computerised long range radar. During 1992 849A flight will be embarked in HMS INVINCIBLE and 849B in HMS ARK ROYAL. 849HQ acts as a training and trials unit at RNAS CULDROSE.

HC 4

Role: Commando asault and utility transport.
Crew: 1 pilot and 1 aircrewman.
Armament: Door mounted 7.62mm machine gun.
Squadron Service: 707, 772, 845 and 846 squadrons in commission.
Notes: Capable of carrying up to 27 troops in the cabin or a wide variety of underslung loads up to 8,000lb in weight. 707 squadron is a training unit at RNAS YEOVILTON. 845 and 846 squadrons are bsed at YEOVILTON but able to embark or detach at short notice to support 3 Commando Brigade. The Sea King HC4 has a fixed undercarriage with no sponsons and no radome.

Westland LYNX

Variants: HAS Mk 3 CTS, HAS 3.
Roles: Surface search and strike; anti-submarine strike; SAR.
Engines: 2 x 900hp Rolls Royce GEM BS 360-07-26 free shaft turbines.
Rotor diameter: 42'0" **Length** 39' 1¹/4" **Height** 11' 0" **Max Weight** 9,500lb.
Max Speed: 150 knots. **Crew:** 1 pilot and 1 observer.
Avionics: Ferranti SEA SPRAY radar. Marconi Orange Crop passive ESM equipment.
Armament: External pylons carry up to 4 x SEA SKUA air to surface missiles or 2 x STINGRAY, Mk 46 torpedoes, depth charges, flares or markers.
Squadron Service: 700L, 702, 815 and 829 squadrons in commission.
Notes: 700L is a trials squadron and 702 is a training squadron based at RNAS PORT-LAND. 815, also based at Portland is the parent unit for single aircraft flights that embark in Type 42 destroyers and some classes of frigate, specialising in the surface strike role. 829 squadron parents flights in the Type 22 and other anti-submarine frigates. A version of the Lynx, the AH1, is operated by the Royal Marines Brigade Air Squadron which is based at RNAS Yeovilton and an improved naval version of the Lynx is undergoing development.
(HAS Mk 8) is now flying and undergoing intensive development trials.

Westland GAZELLE HT2

Engine: 1 x 592shp Turbomeca ASTAZOU free power turbine.
Crew: 1 or 2 pilots.
Notes: In service with 705 squadron at RNAS CULDROSE. Used for training all RN helicopter pilots up to "wings standard" before they move onto the Sea King or Lynx. A version of the Gazelle, the AH1, is used by the Royal Marines Brigade Air Squadron based at RNAS Yeovilton.

100

OTHER AIRCRAFT TYPES IN ROYAL NAVY SERVICE DURING 1992

British Aerospace JETSTREAM T2 and T3

Engines: 2 x 940hp Turbomeca ASTAZOU 16D turboprops. (T3 Garrett turboprops).
Crew: 1 or 2 pilots, 2 student observers plus 3 other seats.
Notes: A number of these aircraft are used by 750 squadron at RNAS CULDROSE for training Fleet Air Arm Observers and also by the Heron flight at RNAS Yeovilton.

de Havilland CHIPMUNK

Engine: 1 x 145hp de Havilland Gipsy Major 8 piston engine.
Crew: 2 pilots.
Notes: Used by the RN Flying Grading Flight at Roborough airport near Plymouth (and as such the first aircraft flown by generations of naval aircrew) and by stations flights at RNAS CULDROSE and YEOVILTON.

British Aerospace CANBERRA TT18

Engines: 2 x 6500lb thrust Rolls Royce AVON turbojets.
Crew: 1 pilot and 1 observer.
Notes: Used by the (civilian manned) Fleet Requirements and Aircraft Direction Unit (FRADU) at RNAS YEOVILTON. Canberras provide towed targets for live firings by ships at sea. Only 2 remain in service to be replaced by Falcon aircraft on contract to MOD(N).

Hawker HUNTER T8, GA11, T7 & T8m

Engine: 1 x 7575lb thrust Rolls Royce AVON turbojet.
Crew: T8 1 or 2 pilots. GA11 1 pilot. T7 1 or 2 pilots. T8m 1 or 2 pilots.
Notes: The Royal Navy has used Hunters to train fixed wing pilots since 1958. A number remain in service at RNAS YEOVILTON with the RN flying standards flight and with FRADU who use them as airborne targets for the aircraft direction school. 899 Squadron also use these aircraft as radar trainers for Sea Harrier pilots.

In addition to these aircraft, the following aircraft have naval functions:
CANBERRA T17: Used by 360 joint RN/RAF Squadron for electronic warfare tasks. Based at RAF WYTON.
British Aerospace 125: Two aircraft, owned by the RN are operated by RN aircrew as part of 32 Squadron RAF based at RAF NORTHOLT.
The Fleet Air Arm Historic flight based at RNAS YEOVILTON has a **SWORDFISH, SEAHAWK, FIREFLY and TIGER MOTH** on strength and these are often seen at air displays in the summer months. The future of the Seahawk is in doubt.

Full details of these and many other naval aircraft can be found in the revised edition of AIRCRAFT OF THE ROYAL NAVY SINCE 1945 published by Maritime Books.

At the end of the line ...

Readers may well find other warships afloat which are not mentioned in this book. The majority have fulfilled a long and useful life and are now relegated to non-seagoing duties. The following list gives details of their current duties:

Pennant Number	Ship	Remarks
A134	RAME HEAD	Escort Maintenance Vessel – now Royal Marines Training Ship at Portland
C35	BELFAST	World War II Cruiser Museum ship – Pool of London (Open to the public) Tel: 071-407 6434
D73	CAVALIER	World War II Destroyer Museum Ship at Hebburn Undergoing Restoration
D12	KENT	County Class Destroyer – Sea Cadet Training Ship at Portsmouth. Future "under consideration"
F126	PLYMOUTH	Type 12 Frigate & Oberon class submarine Museum Ships at Birkenhead
S21	ONYX	Open to the public spring 1992. Tel: 051 647 2366
S11	ORPHEUS	Oberon Class Submarine Harbour Training Ship at Gosport
S67	ALLIANCE	Submarine – Museum Ship at Gosport Open to the public. Tel: 0705 - 511485

At the time of publishing the following ships were awaiting tow for scrap or sale.

PORTSMOUTH		MILFORD HAVEN	ROSYTH	PLYMOUTH
Brereton	Kedleston	Eskimo	Dreadnought	Conqueror
Charybdis	Manly	Woodlark	Churchill	Warspite
Endurance	Mentor	(Targets)		
Fawn	Milbrook			
Hecate	Ocelot			
Hubberston	Otter			

A number of merchant ships are on charter to various MOD departments. They include MAERSK GANNET, MAERSK ASCENCION, ST BRANDAN, INDOMITABLE & OIL MARINER & in support of the Falkland Island commitment. NORTHELLA, PROUD SEAHORSE, BRITISH ENTERPRISE IV and NORTHERN HORIZON have hydrographic, training/trials roles in UK waters.

NOTES

PHOTOGRAPHERS

The selection of photographs for use in the next edition will be made in October/ November. We only use pictures of ships underway – preferably without a background. Please send a SAE if you want photographs returned. Readers are welcome to send in proposed alterations/additions to the text at any time.